T0149522

ENRAGED EDNA

A QUEST TO TEACH PEOPLE GOOD MANNERS AND CORRECT BEHAVIOUR

Jose Mylabathula

ENRAGED EDNA
A QUEST TO TEACH PEOPLE GOOD MANNERS AND CORRECT BEHAVIOUR

iUniverse books may be ordered through booksellers or by contacting:

iUniverse
1663 Liberty Drive
Bloomington, IN 47403
www.iuniverse.com
1-800-Authors (1-800-288-4677)

Because of the dynamic nature of the Internet, any web addresses or links contained in this book may have changed since publication and may no longer be valid. The views expressed in this work are solely those of the author and do not necessarily reflect the views of the publisher, and the publisher hereby disclaims any responsibility for them.

Any people depicted in stock imagery provided by Thinkstock are models, and such images are being used for illustrative purposes only.
Certain stock imagery © Thinkstock.

ISBN: 978-1-5320-3619-4 (sc)
ISBN: 978-1-5320-3620-0 (hc)
ISBN: 978-1-5320-3621-7 (e)

Library of Congress Control Number: 2017916741

Print information available on the last page.

iUniverse rev. date: 01/12/2018

I would like to introduce you to a woman named Edna.

Edna is known as Enraged Edna by a number of people.

Edna had become enraged from people who did not have the wonderful, and perfect understanding of how to treat other people in the kind ways that she did.

Edna had also become enraged about people who were not behaving in the correct ways that she did.

During one morning Edna decided to start a quest to teach people what good manners and correct human behaviour are.

Edna knew that her opportunity to start teaching people good manners and correct behaviour could begin anywhere she went.

Edna decided to start
her quest by going
to a local coffee
shop to buy a cup of
tea, and possibly a
sweet pastry snack,
to energize herself
to become strong
enough to focus her
mind on teaching her
perfect way of being
to other people.

Edna arrived to the local coffee shop, walked to the shop's front entrance door while she sang the country's national anthem, opened the door, and the following occurred:

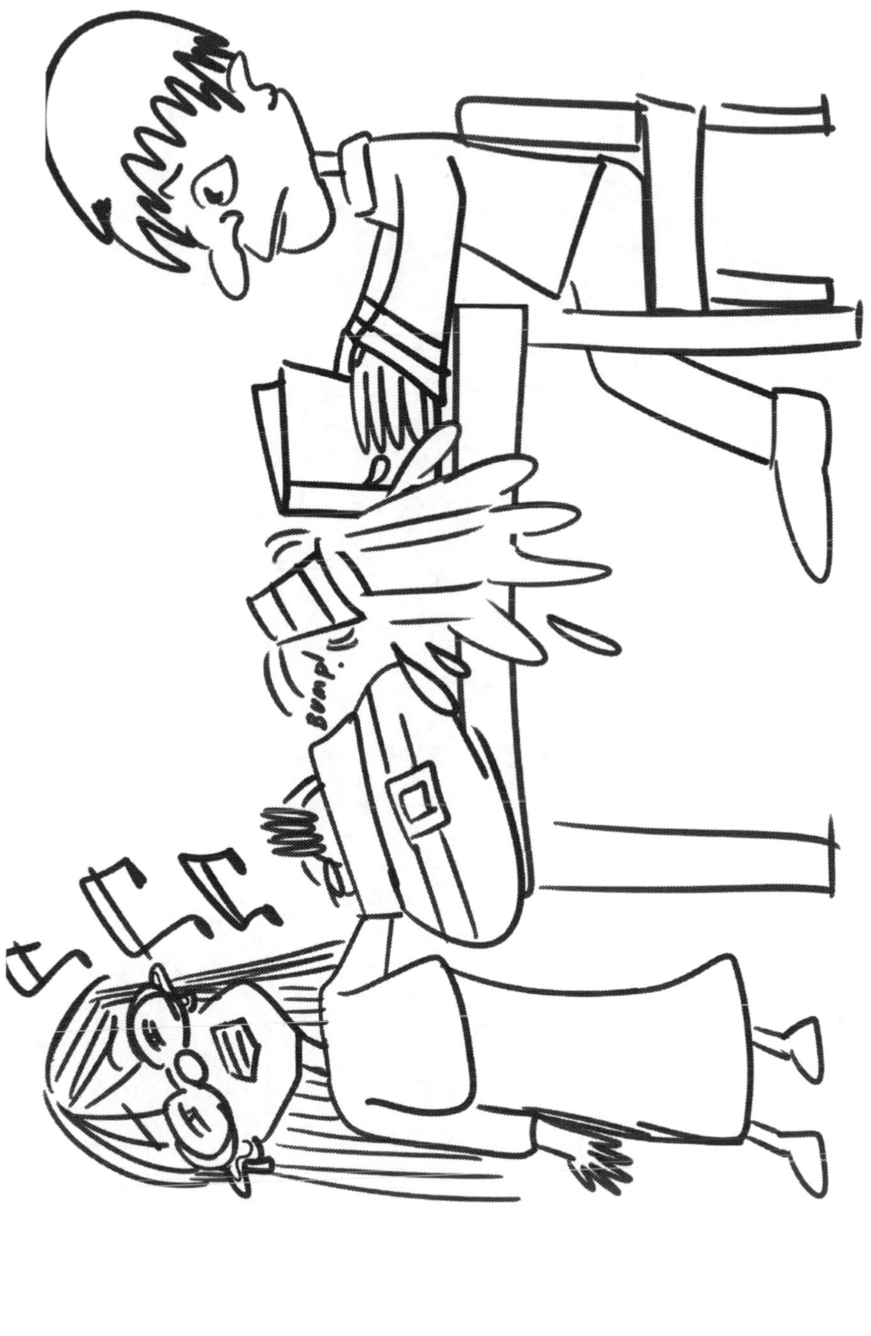
Bump!

Enraged Edna suddenly erupted and said,

Exhausted from the lesson she had just taught the man in the coffee shop, Edna calmed down and decided to go to the public library to enjoy some peace and quiet until lunchtime.

The main rule of a public library is that people must keep their voices down to maintain a quiet atmosphere, so Edna knew that the library would be a good place for her to be able to relax for a while.

Edna found a place in the public library to sit by herself, then her cellular phone started to ring.

Enraged Edna suddenly erupted and said,

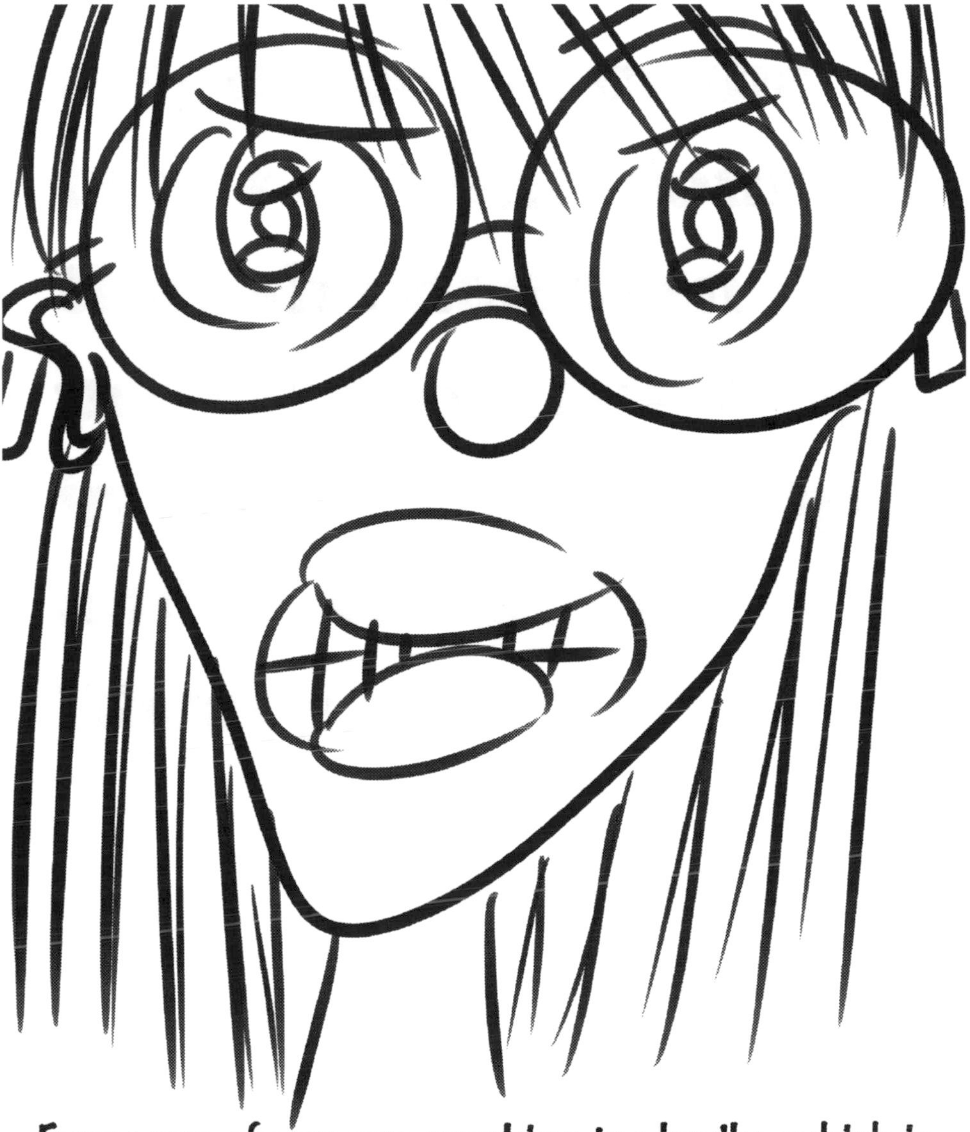

Every one of you are speaking too loudly, which is against the library's rules! You're even making it too difficult for me to hear the person speaking on my speaker phone!

Edna thought it would be a good idea to go shopping, because the fun she would have spending money could erase the disgusting feeling she had just acquired from witnessing the behaviour of the people at the coffee shop and the public library.

Edna walked into a large clothing store and suddenly saw some clothes that she thought may possibly look great with a red jacket that she had at home.

Unfortunately, the large clothing store did not have any red jackets for Edna to test how a red jacket would look with the clothing in the store.

Edna had an idea spark within her mind, and then the following occurred:

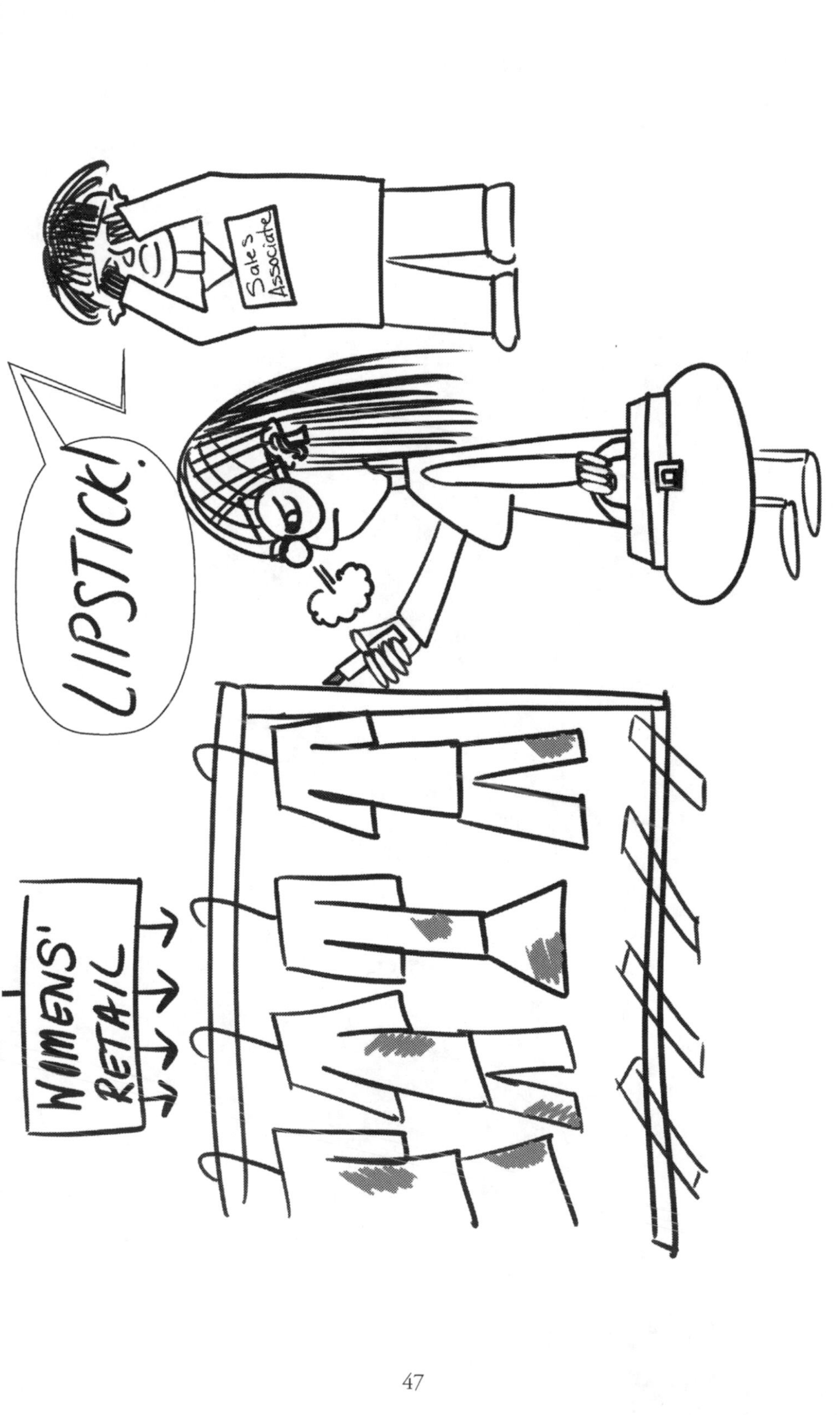
LIPSTICK!
WOMENS' RETAIL
Sales Associate

**Enraged Edna
suddenly erupted
and said,**

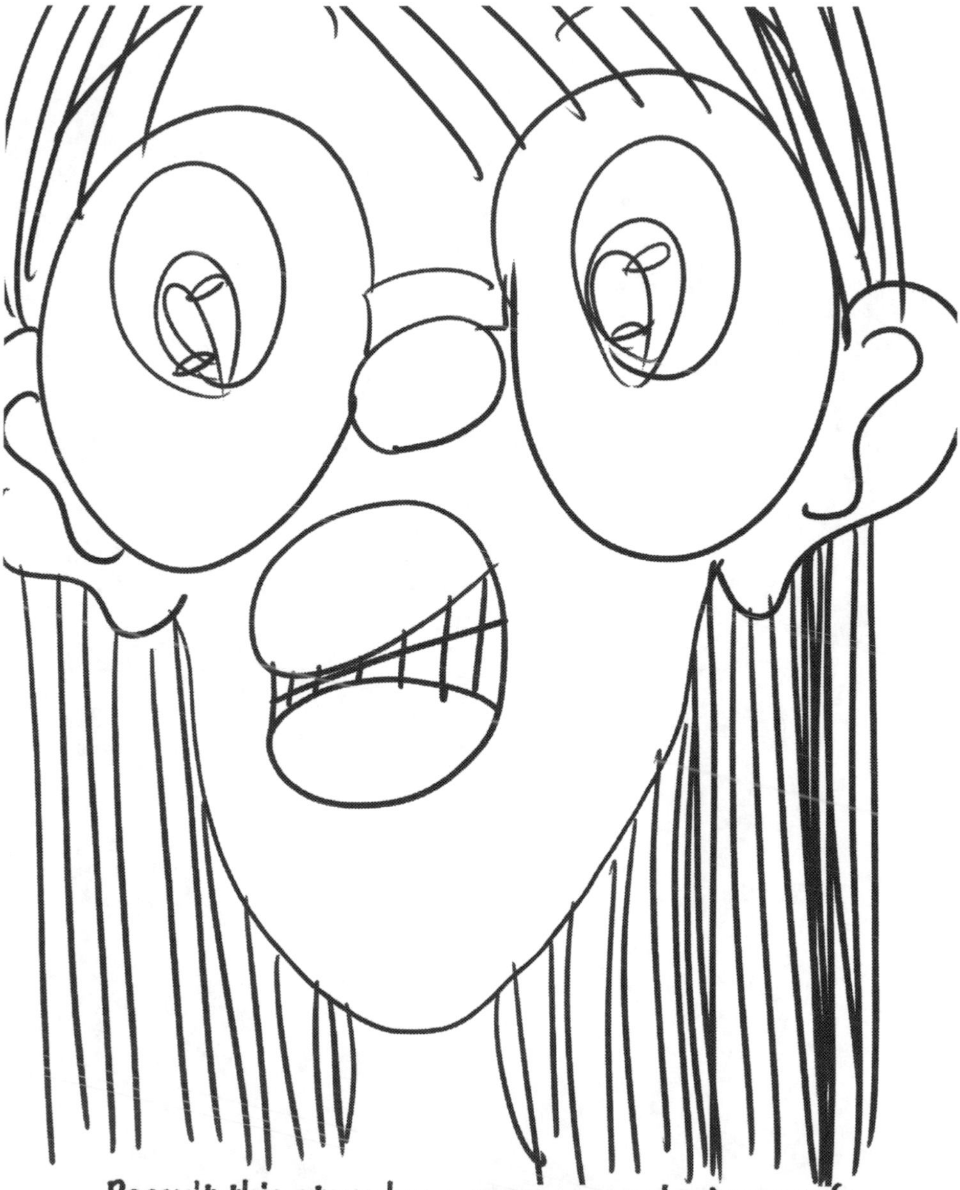

Doesn't this store have more convenient ways for shoppers to find out what other colours would match the fashion products they have for sale here?

Edna was beginning to lose her patience with peoples' incorrect behaviour, so she left the clothing store to avoid getting angry in an obvious way that others could have found strange.

Edna walked on a sidewalk at a casual pace.

While Edna was walking on the sidewalk the following occurred:

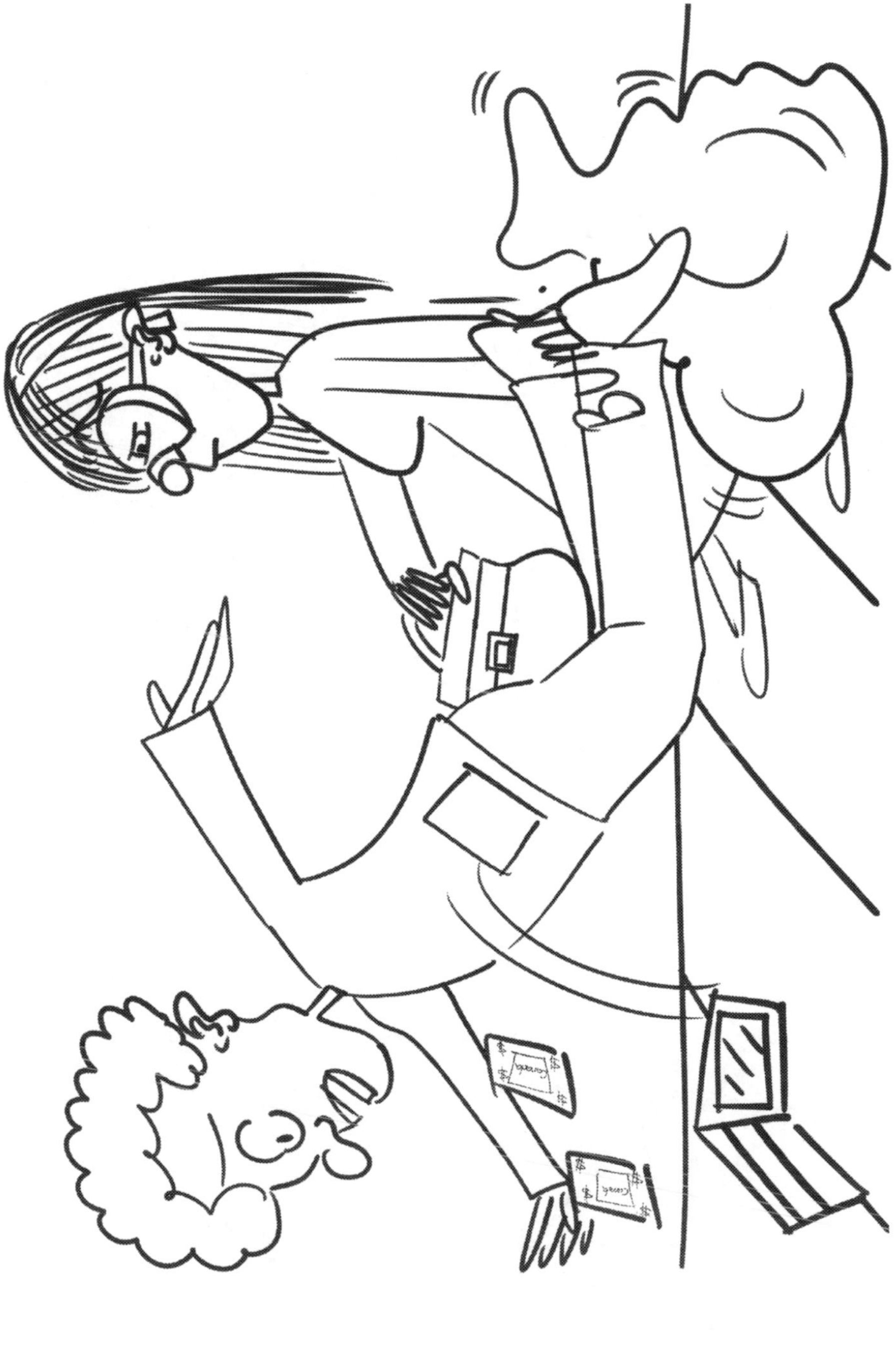

Enraged Edna suddenly erupted and said,

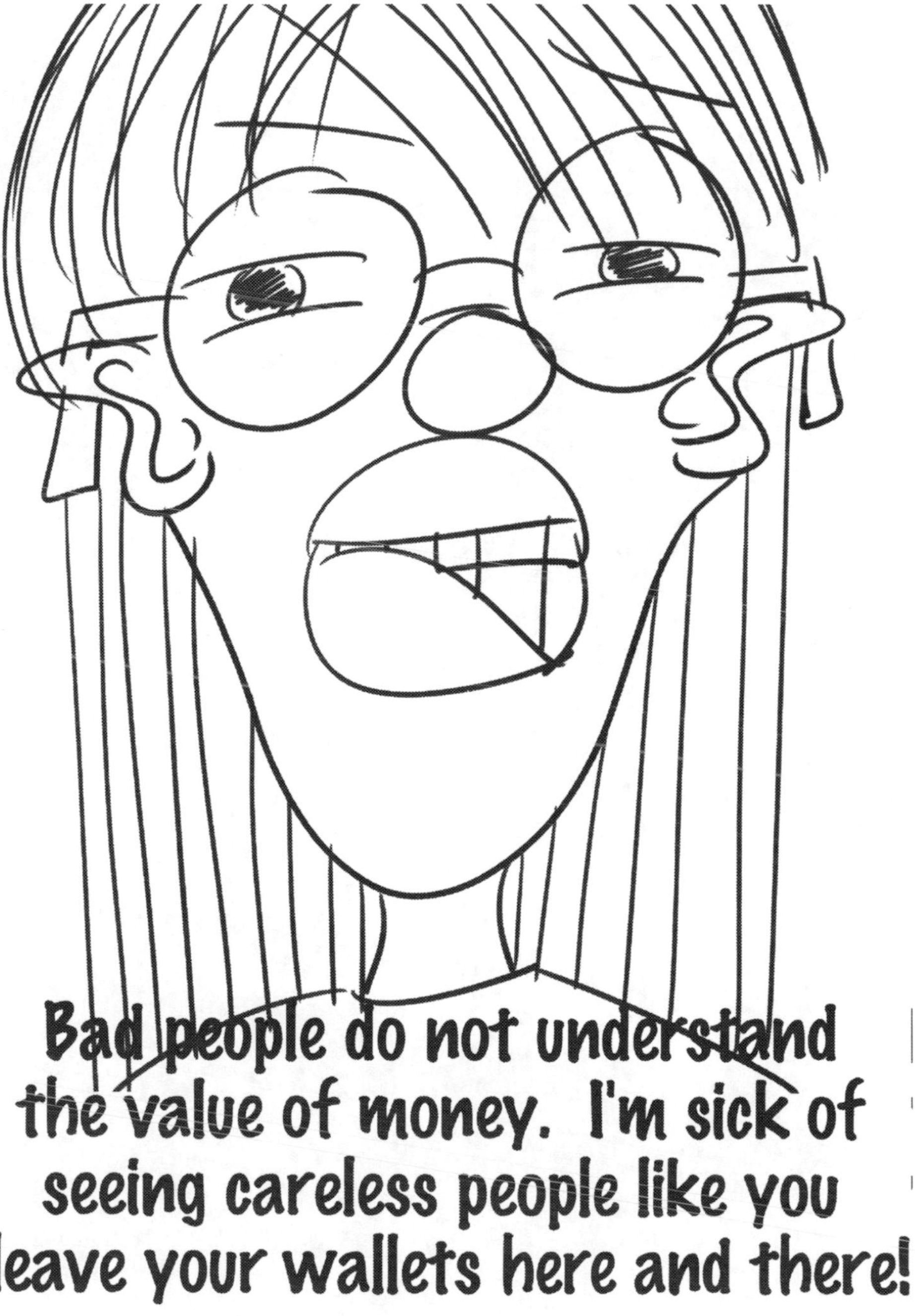
Bad people do not understand the value of money. I'm sick of seeing careless people like you leave your wallets here and there!

Edna had started to notice that there was an urgent need from society for her to teach people good manners and correct behaviour, and her motivation towards continuing her quest increased.

Edna started to feel stressed out from suddenly realizing how incredibly important her existence in the world was, and she decided to continue walking on the sidewalk to calm down from this unexpected realization about herself.

As Edna continued to walk on the sidewalk the following occurred:

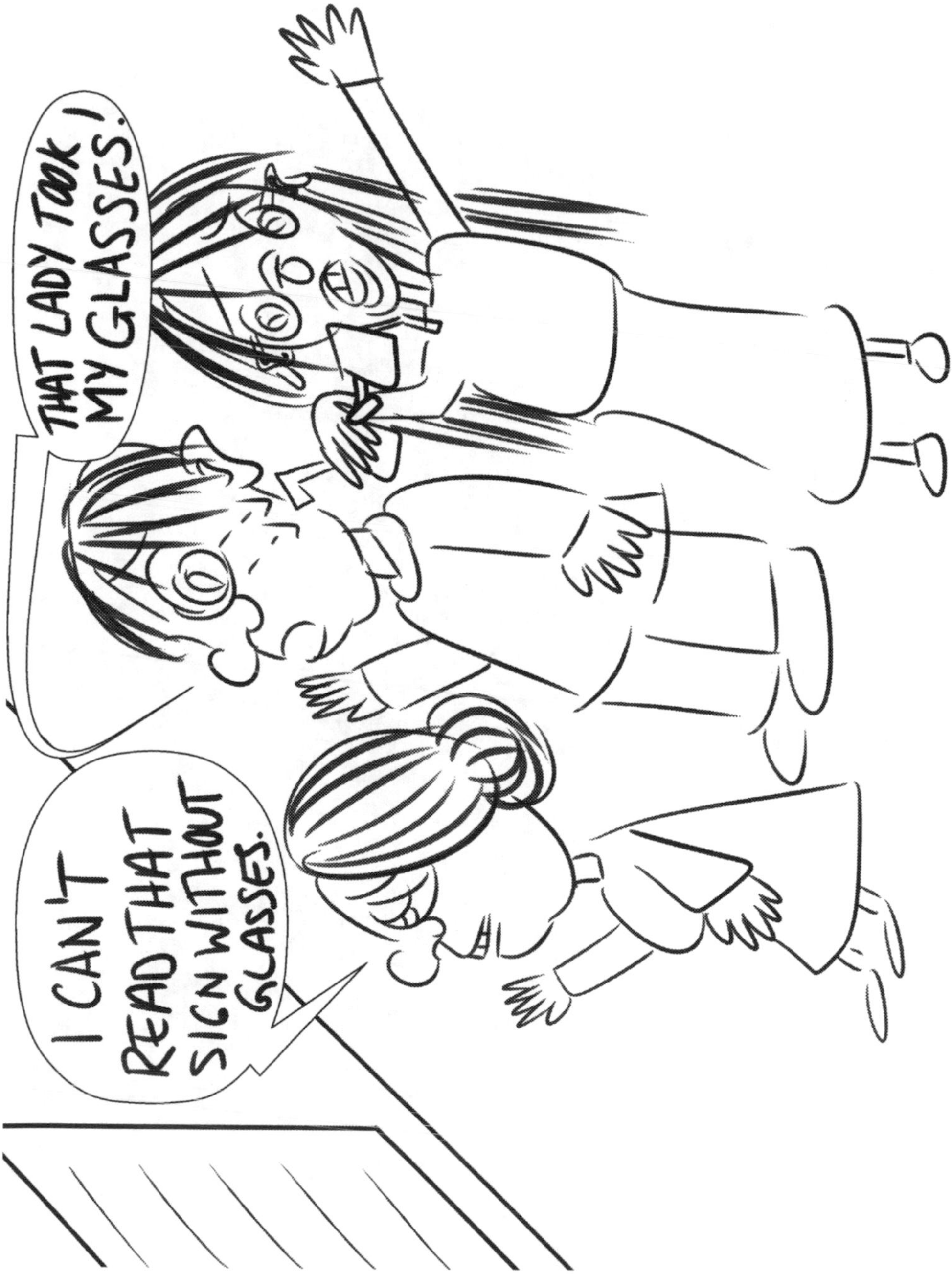
I CAN'T READ THAT SIGN WITHOUT GLASSES.
THAT LADY TOOK MY GLASSES!

**Enraged Edna
suddenly erupted
and said,**

Get out of the way so that I can assist that elderly woman
who has a visual impairment! You should make yourself more
aware about how difficult it is to read with
a visual impairment sir!

After assisting that elderly lady with finding reading glasses, Edna suddenly remembered that she needed to buy new sunglasses.

Edna knew that she should keep her eyes in good health for her to be able to locate other possible teaching opportunities, therefore purchasing new sunglasses to protect her eyes from the sunshine became a quest necessity.

Edna tried on new sunglasses in a sunglasses store and the following occurred:

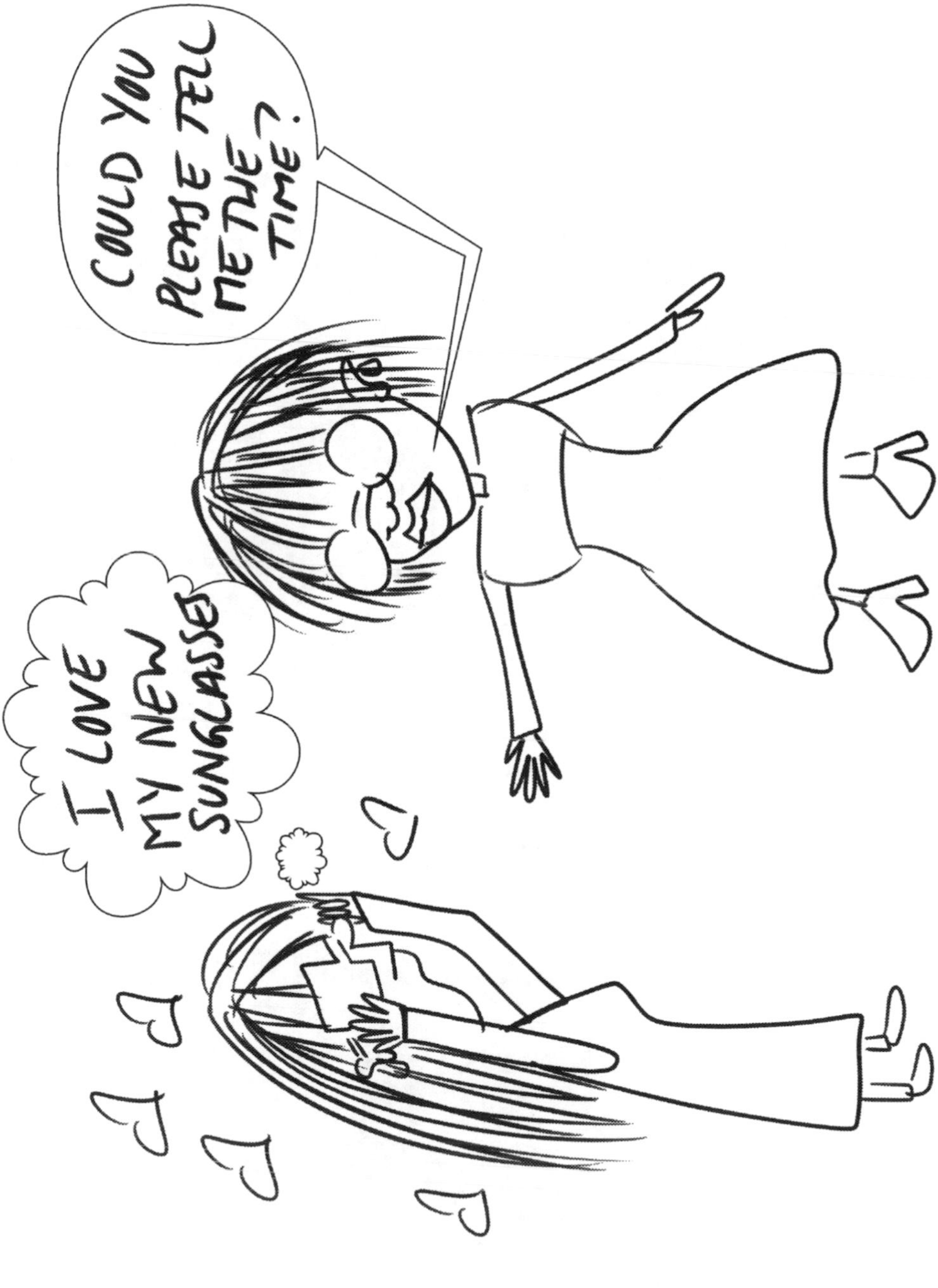
I LOVE MY NEW SUNGLASSES
COULD YOU PLEASE TELL ME THE TIME?

**Enraged Edna
suddenly erupted
and said,**

Can't you remove your sunglasses
when you are speaking to me?
It is rude to not allow me to see
your eyes when we are speaking
to each other.

After purchasing her new sunglasses Edna put her newly purchased important tool towards protecting her eyes in her purse and exited the store.

**As Edna walked
out of the store the
following occurred:**

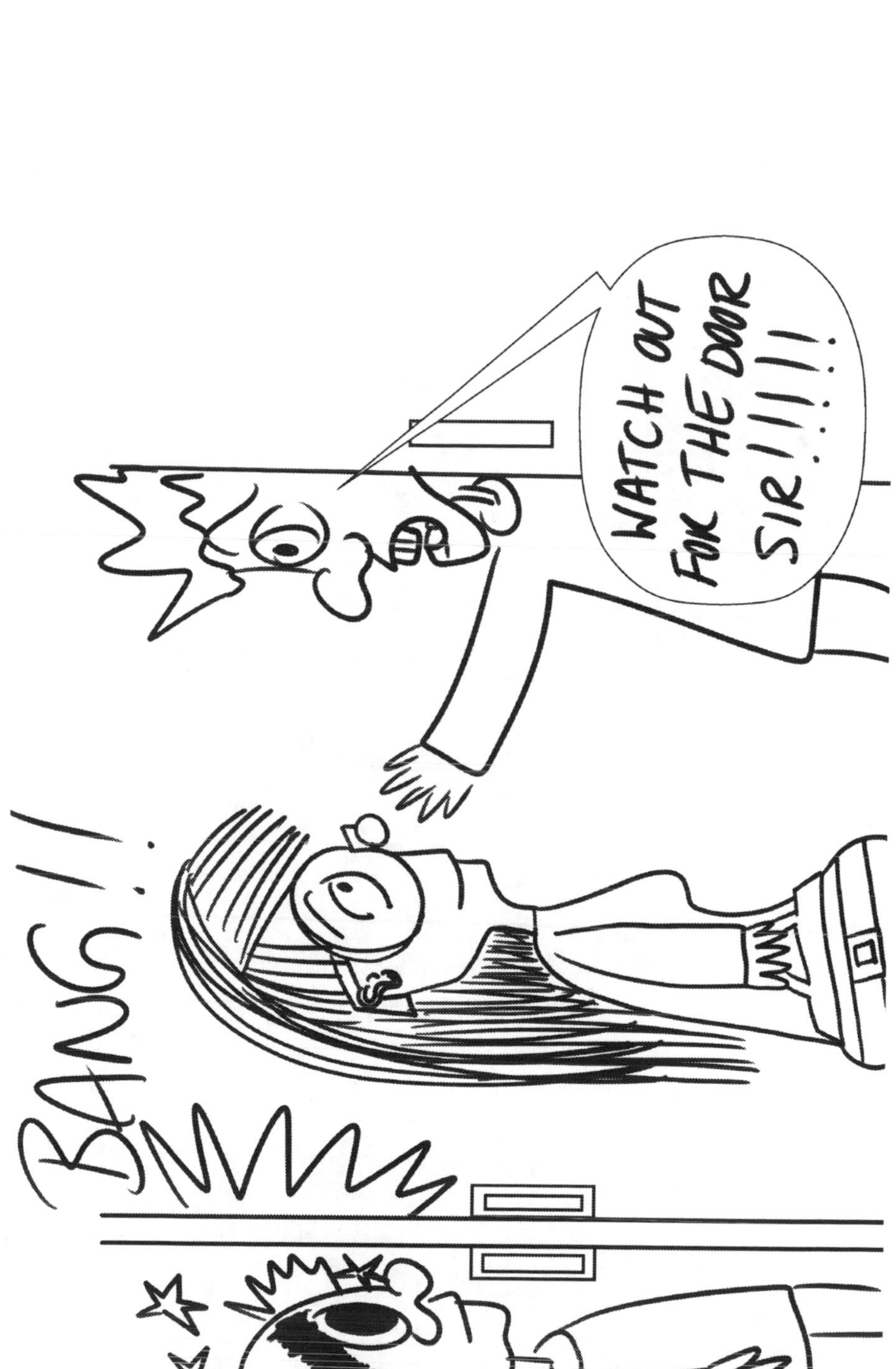
WATCH OUT FOR THE DOOR SIR!!!!!!...
BANG!!

**Enraged Edna
became happy and
said,**

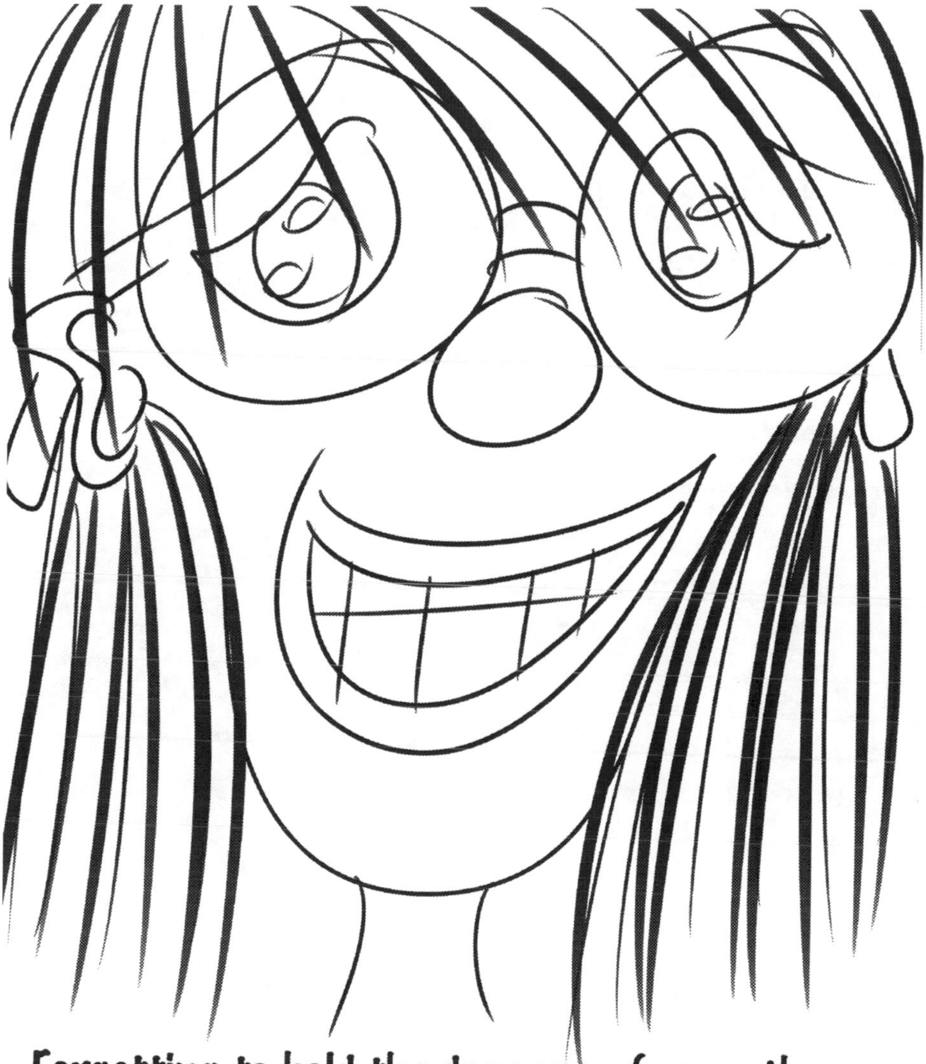

Forgetting to hold the door open for another person is such bad manners.
It's nice to know people like you are as considerate for others as I am.

Edna decided to go home to rest from the first day of her teaching quest.

Edna was excited from finding her purpose in life, got ready for bed, and fell asleep.